Cryptocurrency

A Step By Step Guide To Investing In Cryptocurrencies
"Unlocking The Digital Frontier"

*(Strategies For Automated Day Trading In Cryptocurrency
That Are Unbelievably Profitable)*

Lúcio Venturi

TABLE OF CONTENT

Introduction

Mining cryptocurrencies: what does it entail?

It takes a powerful combination of hardware and software to mine cryptocurrency, and you need both to get started. Because the value of a currency is dependent on the number of units of that currency that are available on the market, the process that determines how many units of currency are available should be extremely closely monitored and very reliable. Mining a cryptocurrency refers to the process of creating new units of that cryptocurrency. It's as simple as that.

In order for you to get a better grasp on it, let's imagine a major national economy that has trillions of dollars deposited throughout all of its banks. Now, because it is not physically possible to store all of the currency notes in banks, they store them in a digital format with a central reserve bank. This allows them to keep track of all of the currency notes. The reserve bank keeps a digital record of what it owes to which bank but does not keep the note in a physical form. This record is kept separate from the note itself. When it needs to inject more money into the economy but does not have enough notes, it will "simply get" those notes printed.

The concerned reserve bank can print as many notes as it can, but it does not do so on its own for no reason even though it has the ability to print as many notes as it can. This is due to the fact that the printing of additional currency and the introduction of additional money into the market does not make individuals richer; rather, it only devalues the currency that is already in circulation and causes inflation. When there are more units of a currency in circulation in a market, the value of that currency becomes more fragmented.

The same thing may be said for cryptocurrency. Mining cryptocurrency is a process that is carefully managed to ensure that the value of the existing units does not decrease. This is done so that new units do not dilute the value of the existing ones.

The price of a cryptocurrency can be determined using the following:

Although the market values of different cryptocurrencies can vary greatly, one characteristic that they all share is their liquidity. The value of cryptocurrency is subject to significant swings at the present time.

Demand and supply are the two primary factors that determine the price of a cryptocurrency, just like they are for almost any other good and service. The value of a certain cryptocurrency goes up when there is a high demand for it but a limited supply of that cryptocurrency. After that, additional units are mined in order to keep the flow going. However, many people have decided to limit the total number of ores that can be mined. For example, the total number of Bitcoins that can ever exist will be capped at 21 million at the current time.

After being mined or exchanged, you could be forgiven for wondering how these cryptocurrencies are kept safe. The answer to this problem is referred to as a wallet. In the context of cryptocurrencies, the term "wallet" can refer either to a collection of private keys that can be used to transfer and receive coins or to software that is designed to hold individual units of a cryptocurrency. Wallets are able to be run as a desktop application or as a service that is hosted on the internet. Since cryptocurrency stored on desktop programs may be accessed even when the user is not connected to the internet, many people find this method to be more convenient. Wallets for cryptocurrencies can come in a wide variety of forms, and each of these forms has its own set of benefits and drawbacks. A wallet's location can be

4

determined by inspecting its address, which is a string of arbitrary characters.

What kind of wallet would be best for you to carry? First and foremost, you need to think about the environment in which you will be using cryptocurrencies. If you are using bitcoin for trading and investing, you may want to explore temporarily holding your coins online on exchanges that have been specifically designed for trading and investing. If you are using cryptocurrencies for these purposes, you can read more about this topic here. When you're not actively trading or investing, the best place for your cryptocurrency holdings to be is in "cold storage." This refers to keeping your bitcoin on a desktop application that offers both online and offline access to its contents. When you keep your cryptocoins online, you run the danger of losing access to your private keys or of the online service suddenly going offline for unknown reasons. Both of these scenarios are possible. If you are merely holding onto your cryptocurrencies and not trading or investing, it is best to store your cryptocoins in cold storage on desktop wallet software. This is because cold storage is less vulnerable to theft than other types of storage. This kind of wallet software is included with the initial Bitcoin client, however there are separate wallet applications available for every distinct kind of cryptocurrency.

Typically ranging from 26 to 35 characters in length, addresses are identifiers that fall into this range. When sending and receiving cryptocurrencies such as Bitcoin, addresses are utilized as the destination of the transaction. A cryptocurrency address can be thought of in a manner that is analogous to a bank account number or a routing number. An address for a cryptocurrency can only ever be used once, in contrast to account and routing numbers. The generation of new addresses, whether done online or offline, is thankfully a simple process. The act of sending and receiving cryptocurrency is automatically considered to be anonymous due to the fact that these arbitrary characters are not associated with any particular person's identify or institution. Once a cryptocurrency address has been used, it must be replaced with a new address that has been randomly created; this is because cryptocurrency addresses cannot be used to identify a specific person or organization. Because of this anonymity, as well as the security provided by blockchain technology, using cryptocurrencies is a trustworthy way to transmit and receive money.

The anonymity provided by cryptocurrencies is extremely vital to the industry as a whole. Bitcoin, the first blockchain-based cryptocurrency, was designed with the goal of making it possible for individuals and organizations to send and receive monetary transactions without the involvement of a central authority in the transaction process. An exchange for cryptocurrencies does not need either party to disclose any personal or identifying information. The anonymity that cryptocoins provide is extremely helpful in settings where data protection is of the utmost importance. Because the transaction takes place solely between the two users concerned, there is no longer a requirement for a traditional financial institution to handle the transfer of funds. Since there is no requirement for a financial institution, the only item that needs to be sent in order to complete the transaction is the value that is being exchanged.

As a quick reminder, here is what we have learnt about blocks, including their significance in cryptocurrencies and the structure of blockchains. We also gained an understanding of the distinctive cryptographic procedure that is used to first create a block and then link subsequent blocks together. We have investigated the concept behind the distributed ledger as well as the significance it plays in the realm of cryptocurrencies. Furthermore, we have gained an understanding of how the mining process works as well as the value that it offers. We analyzed the concept of a cryptocurrency wallet, which is built on top of blockchain technology and distributed ledgers. In addition to this, we investigated whether kinds of cryptocurrency wallets are appropriate for use in various scenarios. In the last part of our investigation, we looked at how significant it is that users of cryptocurrency systems have the ability to remain anonymous. It is time to investigate the fresh and interesting history that lies behind cryptocurrencies like bitcoin and ethereum.

The Dangerous Triangle Of Symmetry

We have examined ascending and descending triangles, both of which have the potential to provide a useful trading indication. However, there are situations when the trendlines come together to form a triangle with symmetry. When the two lines intersect, there will be a point at which something must take place since the highs are becoming lower and the lows are growing higher. The problem with this formation is that it involves an extremely high level of danger. There is a 50% chance that it will go up, and there is a 50% chance that it will go down. However, I would think that it will be around 90% fast and furious.

Trading in a market that does not have a distinct trend can be challenging, as I have emphasized on multiple occasions. The trend is your friend. If there is a really excellent strong moving average line, for instance, in which case you have a 50–60% chance that the breakout will be in the same direction, you have a trendless market if one trendline is going up and the other is going down and the symmetrical triangle is there. And by definition, when you have a market with these two trendlines, you have a trendless market. On the other hand, there is a significant likelihood that there will be a fakeout first (which will typically have low volume, whilst the actual breakout will see an increase in trading volume).

If you are going to take a risk on one of these triangles, it is probably best to wait until the breakout and the new trend become evident. In the meantime, make sure to maintain your stop-loss orders tight, as the price may run away from you in the opposite direction. In point of fact, prices fairly frequently gap up (or down) from these formations, which means that even your stop-loss may not be of any assistance to you.

Your aim for the amount of profit you want to make can be calculated by adding the point at which the triangle broke out to the point at which it was at its deepest point when it first began to develop. Your stop-loss order ought to be placed at the most recent level at which the price achieved contact with the triangle's base line. Given that this pattern has a probability of between 50 and 60%, you will need a risk-to-reward ratio that is greater than 2:1 for it to have any chance of turning a profit for you. Personally, I wouldn't bet on anything with odds lower than 4:1.

If you look at the moving average, though, you will be able to ride the trend. As long as the price remains higher than the 20–50-day moving average, you can continue to move forward with your trade and bring your stop-loss order into alignment with the moving average on a daily basis. If you do it this way, you'll be instantly stopped out of the game if the trend changes. A trailing stop similar to this one is an excellent approach to manage a position held for a longer period of time.

MACD stands for "moving average convergence/divergence."

One of the most popular bitcoin techniques is known as the MOVING AVERAGE CONVERGENCE/DIVERGENCE (MACD) strategy. The reason for this is because it typically offers an early and distinct indicator when a reversal may take place as the lines begin to turn, ultimately validating the cue when a crossover takes place.

The Moving Average Convergence and Divergence (MACD) is an example of a trend-following indicator that shows whether or not the short-term price momentum is moving in the same direction as the long-term price momentum. In circumstances in which it does not continue to go in the same direction, then it is utilized to forecast whether or not a trend change is unavoidable. There are four elements that make up the MACD cryptocurrency strategy: the ZERO LINE, the MACD LINE, the SIGNAL LINE, and the HISTOGRAM.

The Positives and Negatives of Using MACD in Business

One of the most popular and commonly used indicators for technical analysis is the moving average convergence/divergence (MACD) indicator, which was developed by Gerald Appel in the late 1960s. This indicator is classified as a lagging indicator.

Using this method, traders are better able to anticipate when a shift in the trend will occur. It uses a histogram to assist traders further, providing them with a visual depiction of the strength of a trend, so clearly defining any crossovers. It gives signals that are very simple to interpret, and it makes any crossovers very evident. However, due to the fact that MACD is a lagging indicator, it is possible for it to give misleading readings, which can have a significant impact on traders if they take positions before they have been validated.

Bollinger Bands are referred to as.

In the 1980s, a financial analyst named John Bollinger was the brains behind the technique. Since that time, traders have employed the instrument for the purpose of performing technical analysis. It functions as an oscillator calculator, which helps to determine whether the market is experiencing low or high volatility, as well as whether or not oversold and overbought situations are present.

The major purpose of this indicator is to indicate how prices are distributed throughout a number that is considered to be average. The three components that make up Bollinger Bands are referred to as the LOWER BAND, the UPPER BAND, and the MOVING AVERAGE LINE. The two outer bands adjust in response to the price action in the market.

When the volatility grows, they move farther away from the middle band, also known as expanding, and when the volatility drops, they move closer to the middle band, also known as contracting.

In the standard formulation of Bollinger Bands, the centerline is represented by a 20-day Simple Moving Average (SMA). When it comes to the upper and lower bands, both of these are determined by computing them depending on the volatility of the market.

20-day Simple Moving Average plus (20-day Standard Deviation times 2) = Upper Band

The Simple Moving Average of 20 Days

Lower Band Formula: 20-day Simple Moving Average minus (20-day Standard Deviation multiplied by 2)

In this configuration, the majority of the price data, at least 85 percent of it, moves in the middle of the lower and upper bands.

However, this data can still be changed depending on the requirements of various trading methods and the various trading techniques themselves.

The Positives and Negatives of Using Bollinger Bands

When used in conjunction with candlesticks, price chart patterns, and other technical indicators, the Bollinger Bands indicator can be a useful component of a cryptocurrency trading strategy that is also successful. Traders make use of this instrument to ascertain whether or not a certain currency (or commodity) is going to reach the highest point during a run, or whether or not it is likely to reach the lowest point during a selloff.

This tactic, despite the fact that it is quite brilliant, does not, regrettably, work perfectly. There is no way to apply Bollinger Bands as if they were a one-size-fits-all trading method. It merely gives traders of cryptocurrencies an indicator of whether a particular digital currency is currently undervalued or overvalued relative to other cryptocurrencies. In addition, given that the strategy makes use of SMA, it gives equal weight to both new and previous trades.

In practice, this has the effect of making the shifts in the market's current position less noticeable. In addition, if the Simple Moving Average (SMA) is set to 20 days, it is possible to obtain a result that is inconsistent, which makes it even more difficult to develop accurate predictions without the assistance of other indicators.

How Many Different Categories Of Miners Are There?

It seems likely that Satoshi, the individual or group credited with the creation of Bitcoin, mined bitcoins on his home computer all by himself in the very beginning. He was the only owner of the entire hashrate. Over the course of time, additional miners joined, resulting in a split of the hashrate and, consequently, the payouts. As cryptocurrency mining gained popularity, the machines used for mining got increasingly sophisticated and specialized in their functionality. Due to the fact that computers have gotten so tremendously specialized in recent years, standard computers can no longer be used effectively for performing such massive amounts of calculations. An outline of the following mining equipment is as follows:

Depending on how many megahertz (MHz) it has, the Central Processing Unit (CPU) in your typical desktop computer or laptop will have a hashrate ranging from 1 to 3 million per second. It may seem like a lot, but if you calculate the odds of winning based on the total hashrate that is now in place, you will find that the amount of money you would spend on electricity to run the computer would far exceed the amount of money you would receive from the awards. Even if the electricity were completely free, you would still run your computer into the ground long before you would see any kind of significant money.

The next step was GPU mining, which stands for Graphics Processing Unit mining. Using your graphical processor is a lot more effective because it has been discovered that these units are considerably more efficient in solving hashes when comparing hashing output with time and electrici-ty cost. This means that using your graphical processor is a lot more effective. Hashrates ranging from

30 to 50 million per second are typical of many Radeons, for instance. That is approximately twenty times more efficient than a typical central processing unit. This is due to the fact that a central processing unit (CPU) must be versatile enough to perform a wide variety of different tasks, whereas a graphics processor is already more specialized.

Application-specific integrated circuits, or ASIC miners, are computers that are designed to hash data at a pace that is higher than that of any other type of computer. That is the only option open to them. You can toss them out of use if they are unable to hash Bitcoin block headers. Consider the following: there are companies who invest millions of dollars into factories that create nothing but ASIC machines for mining. This is their entire business plan, and it generates a significant amount of revenue. For instance, the business Bitmain, which is responsible for the creation of the well-known Antminer and owns the majority of the Bitcoin miner output, is most likely worth a billion dollars. These ASIC miners are capable of performing many giga, and even occasionally tera, hashes per second. One giga equals one billion, and one tera equals one trillion. These are ridiculously enormous amounts of money. However, blockchains like Ethereum and many others are working to keep the mining within the capabilities of GPUs. This prevents the construction of any specialized machinery, ensuring that decentralization is maintained to its full potential.

Swing Trading Includes Both Positive And Negative Aspects

1. Swing trading does not need to be your full-time occupation: anyone who possesses the necessary information and investment cash can try their hand at it. Because trades take place over a longer period of time (from days to weeks rather than minutes and hours), they do not require constant monitoring. A person who engages in swing trading can even maintain a different job throughout the day (so long as they do not check their trading screens frequently while at work).

2. The possibility of significant advantages: Keeping a trade open for a number of days or weeks may bring about larger rewards than trading in and out of the same security on multiple occasions throughout the course of a single trading day. Trades, for the most part, need time to work out before they can be profitable.

3. The swing trader doesn't need to keep constant watch because they can make sure their stop losses are in place. Even though there is a possibility that a stop order will be carried out at a terrible value, using a stop order is preferable to the constant examination of each vacant position that is required in day trading.

4. Lower levels of pressure and the risk of burnout As a result of the fact that swing trading is only occasionally an all-day job, there is a much reduced risk of burnout brought on by high levels of strain. The majority of people who engage in swing trading also have a day job or some other source of income, which allows them to compensate for, or at least reduce the impact of, their trading losses.

5. Swing trading shouldn't involve a significant financial commitment and should be possible with just one computer and the standard trading instruments. There is no need for the cutting-edge innovation that is required for day trading.

Several Fallacies Regarding Cryptocurrencies And Blockchain Technology

During the craze around Bitcoin in 2017, a number of common misunderstandings regarding the industry as a whole became more widespread. These errors may have been a factor in the subsequent drop in the price of bitcoin that followed the increase. It is essential to keep in mind that blockchain technology, as well as the market for cryptocurrencies as a direct result of it, are still in their infancy, and things are progressing at a rapid pace. Permit me to dispel some of the most widespread misconceptions, which are as follows:

The Only People Who Should Use Cryptocurrencies Are Criminals.

One of the most important aspects of several cryptocurrencies is their ability to maintain users' anonymity. That is to say, no one will be able to determine who you are when you carry out transactions. In addition, other cryptocurrencies, unlike bitcoin, are built on a decentralized blockchain. This implies that they are not solely under the jurisdiction of a centralized government. Despite the fact that law-abiding citizens of corrupt nations might benefit from these cryptocurrencies as well, criminals are drawn to them due to the qualities described above. For instance, if you do not trust the bank in your home country or the government of that country due to political unrest or corruption, investing in blockchain and cryptocurrency assets may be the most effective approach to keep your money secure.

Transactions in any cryptocurrency can be made completely anonymous.

For whatever reason, a lot of people connect Bitcoin with remaining anonymous online. Bitcoin, on the other hand, and the vast majority of other cryptocurrencies, do not support any kind of anonymity. The public blockchain is updated with a record of every transaction that takes place with these currency. Anonymity is a feature that is valued by some cryptocurrencies, such as Monero. This means that no one outside of the transaction can determine the source, amount, or destination of the transaction. The vast majority of other forms of cryptocurrency, including Bitcoin, do not function in this way.

The only application of blockchain technology now available is bitcoin.

Bitcoin and other cryptocurrencies are an unimportant byproduct of the change brought about by blockchain technology. There is a widespread misconception that Satoshi Nakamoto created Bitcoin for no other reason than to illustrate how blockchain technology can function. That is the furthest thing possible from the truth. However, there is a possibility that blockchain technology will be beneficial to virtually every sector and organization in the globe.

Witness who is disconnected.

There is a possibility that Separated Witness (SegWit) is a test of a brittle fork. Pieter Wuille, co-founder of Blockstream, and architect Pieter Wuille both urged disconnected Witness to be protected by the end of December 2015. SegWit could be a rewrite aimed at gaining a better understanding of transaction malleability, an issue that has been referred to be a weakness in bitcoin's security. Separated Witness is an option that might be available to you. Tom's examination of which individuals' signatures make up the majority of the data would, in the end, cause a disconnect between it and data pertaining to different transactions. In addition to having two different kinds of an impact, the condition that Disengaged Witness have been prescribed similarly a response in proper order about scalability. An user-activated fragile fork, also known as a UASF, is a flawed possibility that investigates how will perform a blockchain upgrade that is not underpinned by means of the individuals that give for worthwhile the network's hashing energy. An UASF will be a faulty possibility that studies how will execute a blockchain upgrade that is flawed.

Independent witness racks up the testimony hours by reciting the various stages of the procedure. It alters the manner in which the vast bulk of the data can be set far over each bitcoin bit. A support system is provided by SegWit. In the past, the transaction limit for the same amount of time continued to work perfectly for older versions of bitcoin modifying. It corrects the adaptability of transactions that had been A border will separate bitcoin undertakings. A more straightforward implementation of the lightning system is acknowledged by SegWit.

The profession of Bitcoin.

Bitcoin Cash will be created by carefully splitting off a new blockchain from the original Bitcoin blockchain. This could have happened around December 1st, 2017 (since bit 478559). A rise in the value of bitcoin

(BTC) and bitcoin cash (BCH) was seen among holders of bitcoin as they imitated the behavior of other bitcoin users during the furious schism. Without integrating SegWit, the Bitcoin industry has expanded the bit measurement from one megabyte to eight megabytes. Eventually Tom's investigating the nighttime to one outstanding 2017, BCH requiring the third The majority of funds received came from assertions made during cryptographic currencies (after BTC but excluding Ethereum). The organization of a significant number of cryptocurrency exchanges has been suspended recently, including one that was still active in 2017. In the United States, many were confused about whether Bitcoin cash would be taxable as income or whether it would be exempt from taxation. In addition, a division for property needed to recognise that there was no starting point for people working in the money organization.

It's a SegWit2x.

The digital currency Bitcoin may have been subject to an unreliable fork that was suggested under the name SegWit2x. It's possible that the individuals' work for Disconnected Witness to Outstanding 2017 could have been the best in the very first place. A significant chunk of the validated "New York Agreement" was compromised in favor of those individuals who needed to boost bit measure at an extreme fork for a higher square degree. This was done so that those individuals could force bit degree to SegWit. The folks assert that a significant percentage of SegWit2x will be included in a stable fork that will take place in November 2017, which will increase the blocksize by 2 MB. On November 8, 2017, the persons who were responsible for developing SegWit2x announced that the hard fork that was scheduled to take place around November 16, 2017 might have been canceled for the time being owing to a lack of understanding.

How Are Bitcoins Obtained Through Mining?

In the conventional system of fiat money, it is the responsibility of the government to print money whenever it is necessary for the government. Bitcoins, on the other hand, cannot be reproduced in any way at this time. The first bitcoins were found in 2009. Mining for these Bitcoins will take place on computers all across the world, and they will compete against one another. People all across the world continue to utilize the Bitcoin network to send bitcoins to one another in order to conduct business.

Nobody will be aware of any of these transactions until and until someone actually keeps track of who sends what to whom. Until then, no one will be aware of any of this activity. The Bitcoin network would take care of all of this by compiling a list including the information regarding all of the transactions that were carried out during a predetermined time period.

The term "block" is used to refer to this list. The miner is responsible for verifying and recording all of these transactions in a ledger after they have been completed. The term "blockchain" refers to the list of blocks that are included in this ledger, which itself is comprised of blocks. This can be put to use for investigating any specific transaction that may have taken place between two Bitcoin addresses, and it can be done so in a number of different ways.

The blockchain will be updated to include the newly generated transaction list whenever one is produced. As a result of this, a comprehensive list of the transactions that have taken place across the Bitcoin network will be generated. To ensure that everyone who takes part in a block is informed of everything that is taking place, an up-to-date copy of the block will be provided to them.

However, are you able to depend on this ledger at all times, and is everything stored in a digital format? How can you ensure that this blockchain will not be altered in any way and that it will continue to function as intended? The "miners" enter the picture at this point in the narrative.

After a batch of completed transactions has been compiled into a block, the miners will then subject that block to a specific procedure. They will start with the data that is already included in a block and then apply a mathematical formula or equation to it in order to transform it into something else. The term "hash" refers to the shortened sequence of letters and numbers that appear to be generated at random as the end result of this process.

This hash would be saved in the final block of a blockchain's chain of transactions.

These hashes have a few qualities that make them particularly intriguing. The generation of a hash from all of the data that is included in the blockchain is a very straightforward process. When looking at the hash, however, it is not feasible to determine what the data actually was in the first place. It is simple to generate a hash from a massive quantity of data, and each individual hash has its own identity. Even if only one character is altered in a Bitcoin block, the hash will be rendered invalid as a result.

The hash that is generated by miners takes into account not just the transactions that are contained within a block but also other tidbits of information as well. A good example of such a piece of information is the hash value of the Bitcoin block that came before it on the blockchain.

A digital wax seal is created as a result of the fact that the hash of each block in the blockchain is generated by utilizing the hash of the block that came before it in the chain.

This offers the confirmation that the specific block, as well as every other block that comes after it, is legitimate and that it has not been tampered with in any way. If there has been any manipulation done to it, then the others will be aware of it.

If you tried to fake a transaction by altering the block that is kept within the blockchain, then the hash of that block would change as well. This would make it impossible to verify the authenticity of the phony transaction. If someone were to examine the legitimacy of the transactions in the blockchain by running it through the hashing equation, then the bogus block would be discovered immediately in that case. Because the hash of each block is used to generate the hash of the block that comes after it in the chain, if you tampered with the hash of only one block, it would cause the hashes of the blocks that came after it in the chain to be incorrect.

This would continue right up to the very last link in the chain, at which point all of the blocks would be modified.

What makes Ether unique in comparison to Bitcoin?

As of the year 2021, Ether has surpassed Litecoin to become the second-largest virtual currency by market capitalization, trailing only Bitcoin. The blockchain for Ethereum was introduced on July 30, 2015, whereas Bitcoin was introduced for the first time on January 3, 2009. In contrast to Bitcoin, the total amount of Ethereum tokens does not have a predetermined limit and instead fluctuates and grows in accordance with demand in a continuous manner. It is rather infinite, which results in the Ethereum blockchain being significantly larger than the bitcoin blockchain. It is anticipated that the Ethereum blockchain will continue to overtake the bitcoin blockchain in the period that is still to come.

Another important distinction is the development of what are known as "smart contracts." These are able to be generated if additional codes are incorporated into the transactions that are recorded on the Ethereum blockchain by participants; hence, the network itself contains code that may be executed. Because the blockchain for Bitcoin is merely a ledger of accounts, and the data associated to bitcoin network transactions is mostly used for preserving records, this is not something that is possible within the blockchain.

The creation of a new block on the Ethereum blockchain takes place in a matter of seconds, however the confirmation of a transaction on the bitcoin blockchain can take several minutes. This is yet another point of differentiation. And maybe most importantly, the most significant distinction between the networks can be seen in their overarching goals and objectives. Bitcoin is an alternative to conventional currencies that was developed to function as a peer-to-peer, decentralized payment system. This system is both secure and private. On the other hand, the Ethereum platform was developed with the intention of facilitating and simplifying the creation of contracts and applications. It was never intended for it to serve as an alternative currency or to take the place of other mediums of exchange. Transactions are conducted using ether as the medium of exchange. Instead, the objective of its establishment was to facilitate and monetize the operations of the Ethereum platform, which was the motivation behind its creation.

Due to the fact that Ethereum is compatible with bitcoin and the fact that the two cryptocurrencies were developed for different reasons, it makes no sense for these two cryptocurrencies to compete with one another from the standpoint of functionality. Despite this, however, they do compete for investor dollars due to the fact that they have both attracted enormous amounts of investments from investors.

To Serve Unlawful Purposes

It's not impossible for criminals to exploit cryptocurrencies for their own nefarious ends. Because money is a medium that may serve numerous purposes, there is no reason why using bitcoin should be any different.

When discussing illegal activities, the connotations of the phrases "unregulated" and "decentralized" are altered. Illicit funding, tax evasion, illicit purchasing, and shady business agreements are all forms of "talking the talk" of a free market that is owned by the people. Examining the relevant data is the most productive thing we can do with reference to this subject. Because of the nature of Bitcoin, is it possible for it to be used in illegal activities? Is there a means to exercise control over it that does not involve the involvement of a regulatory body? How much Bitcoin is spent on these activities currently?

There has been some back and forth over the past few years on whether or not the primary purpose of bitcoin is to facilitate unlawful activity. It's possible that one piece will discuss how Bitcoin is used to finance terrorists, while another will claim that this accounts for less than one percent of all Bitcoin transactions. The United Nations (UN) estimates that only between 2% and 5% of the cryptocurrency that is now in circulation worldwide is being used for illegal activities such as money laundering or other forms of criminal activity (2021 Forbes). The question is not whether or whether these things consume a certain percentage of BTC and other cryptocurrencies; rather, the question is whether or not there is room for this exploit to grow and become more widespread.

Ransomware

Ransomware is one of the most typical kinds of online criminal activity that involves Bitcoin. That is the scenario in which a single hacker or a group of hackers get into a computer (or a set of machines, such as the private network of a firm) and demand payment in exchange for returning the data they have stolen. Due to the fact that blockchain-based currencies are inherently anonymous, the ransom is typically requested in the form of Bitcoin or another cryptocurrency. There will be a record of the transfer, but it won't indicate who made it or who received it. It is becoming increasingly difficult for the judicial forces to trace down the perpetrators of the attacks.

The Hidden Web

The "dark web" is another word whose definition may take several pages to fully explain. For the sake of this chapter, we will describe it as a certain area of the internet that can only be accessed by using specialized software and having the appropriate authorizations. Because there are multiple tiers within the dark web, entering is not like walking into a single-floor club. Purchases of illegal goods, such as narcotics, alcohol, prostitution, illegal pornography, and illegal funding, are the most common activities conducted on the dark web. Due to the fact that users can transact in a pseudonymous manner with Bitcoin, there is yet another industry that finds value in utilizing the cryptocurrency.

Misappropriation of Funds

The process of cleaning money obtained through illicit means by using Bitcoin is not too dissimilar to the process of cleaning money obtained through illegal means by using conventional currency. In addition to the anonymity of transactions and the difficulty in determining who the owners of BTC are, the most crucial step in the laundering process is the incorporation of the money into the 'legal' side: Where did that money originate from? Gains in bitcoin were the source of it.

In a similar vein, people are able to build legitimate businesses that accept Bitcoin (BTC) and then use the proceeds of those businesses to launder money. This way, both the placement of the money and its integration into the system can be covered.

Keeping An Eye On Cryptocurrencies And Engaging In Transactions With Them

On certain websites, you'll be able to keep track of the current state of your bitcoin holdings. You can choose to do this manually or automatically depending on your preferences. If you go with the second choice, entering the code that you get from the transaction on the website is as simple as chopping it from your clipboard and pasting it into the appropriate field. After that point, the process will be carried out automatically. You will be kept apprised of the fluctuations that take place on a daily basis.

You will need to first log in before viewing your portfolio after you have created it for yourself and given it a name and a password. That is the extent of the matter. Because of this fantastic advancement, you will be able to keep track of your money even if it is held in a number of different wallets or exchanges. This is a huge benefit. You will also be able to calculate the coin's average price for yourself if you have many separate positions of the same coin. You also have the option of having the tax added to the total, which is in addition to that.

Putting Up for Sale Various Forms of Cryptocurrency

If a trader is able to determine when it is important to get out of a deal, then that trader has the potential to be regarded as having a high level of experience. Because they are waiting for the best time to sell their assets, a sizeable number of traders do not instantly sell their holdings. Instead, they continue to monitor the market. Nevertheless, when would be the best moment to really sell?

It is probable that you shouldn't sell your assets just yet because it has only been relatively recently that virtual currencies have been made available on a global basis. In contrast to equities and other forms of assets, these digital coins, in the same way that one may use the United States Dollar, are immediately usable in the manner in which one would use the currency of the United States. It is not necessary to offer them for sale in order to bring in more money because doing so is not required.

Buying an asset with the purpose of holding on to it as part of one's portfolio is another approach that should be avoided because it is not a good one. It is in your best interest to refrain from hoarding because doing so will cause you to miss out on prospective money. You should make it a goal to earn a profit on occasion in order to increase the diversity of your holdings and make utilization of various other cryptocurrencies.

Let's imagine you were successful in creating a substantial profit, and now you're thinking of placing a stop loss order below it so that you can sell off some of the assets in your portfolio so you can recoup some of your losses.

Keeping track of the ups and downs of your current financial situation can turn out to be profitable for you in the long run. You may decide to trade within such a channel of low and high prices if you do not believe the price will hit a new high. Alternatively, you may choose to trade outside of such a channel. If you completed it in this manner, you would be able to exit close to the top and enter close to the bottom of the room.

Will there ever come a moment when purchasing cryptocurrency would be a complete and utter waste of time?

You should make an investment in cryptocurrencies as soon as you possibly can, or even before the adoption process gets started, if you want to make the most out of the situation. On the other hand, one can always begin investing in digital currency at any point in time. This is something that is always possible. There is a possibility that in the not too distant future, there may be fresh new cryptocurrencies, some of which may have incredibly huge price increases that you will be able to take part in.

It is in everyone's best interest to keep a cheerful attitude, as nobody can truly know what the future holds. You should make the decision to concentrate on the positive potential that using cryptocurrency may provide to you. This decision should be made consciously. Investigate and learn as much as you can about cryptocurrencies through as much research and study as you can manage. The younger generations are well aware of the prospects that may become available for them in the future as a result of the proliferation of bitcoin.

According to Everett Rogers, there are four stages involved in the adoption process, and they are as follows:

They were trailblazers in their industry.

Those Who Came Before Us on the Field

Those who were late to join the majority After the Late Majority

At this point in time, it's very likely that we're still at the Early Adopters stage of the process. Because of this, you still have a big way to go before you can fully utilize digital currency. For instance, a substantial portion of the population does not yet have adequate knowledge of bitcoins. As a result, you should make the best of the current conditions and invest in digital currency before everyone else starts doing so.

When Will Crypto Be Useful?

Enrobed in a purple satin vestment as interesting, eccentric, and colorful as the man himself, Mike Novogratz, the high priest of Crypto, thrilled and delighted his disciples, adherents, and devotees from the main stage of Bitcoin2021 Miami. Confirming what the audience of crypto-revelers already deeply believe, the crypto-billionaire explained, "What gives it [value] is this social construct, that we believe it's got value. It's the narrative. And so we need more and more storytellers, and the optimism is, we're gettin' 'em. (Applause)." Mr. Novogratz has a good reason to believe that crypto is valuable. In March 2021, he revealed that cryptocurrencies made up nearly 85% ($4.8 billion) of his $5.65 billion net worth.

The Problem Is Not One Of Awareness.

Cryptography is a term that is practically familiar to everyone. nonetheless, investing in a new asset class on new trading platforms may be entertaining and interesting; nonetheless, the market valuation of all the cryptocurrencies that have ever been generated equals less than $2 trillion, which is around 0.2% of the estimated total wealth of $1 quadrillion that has been accumulated in the globe. To put it another way, in order for cryptocurrencies to achieve any kind of considerable growth, they are going to need to become as practical and approachable as traditional currencies. This is not a problem of lack of knowledge, nor is it a problem that can be fixed by the use of storytelling. It's a technological problem—a quite significant one, in fact.

Safe while remaining decentralized. Take any two of them.

The promise of decentralized finance, also known as DeFi, is the financial independence made possible by the system's three most important characteristics: its scale, its security, and its decentralization. Sadly, there are a number of substantial technical obstacles that preclude any device from achieving full measurements of all three. In practical terms, this means that your network can either be large and secure, decentralized and secure, or large and decentralized. But it can't be both large and decentralized at the same time.

Visa

Visa estimates that there are over 3.3 billion Visa cards in circulation across the globe, and the global processing network of the corporation, known as VisaNet, is capable of handling more than 65,000 transactions per second. Even while Visa only handles roughly 2,000 transactions per day on average, it is comforting to know that VisaNet wouldn't even flinch if every person on the planet had a Visa card. Visa places a premium on payments that are prompt, safe, and dependable. It is now one of the safest financial networks in the world despite having been expanded up to global levels. However, there is just one location for it.

Bitcoin (BTC)

In contrast, a Bitcoin block that contains between 2,500 and 2,700 transactions is mined around every 10 minutes on average. This equates to approximately 5 tps less. Therefore, it is impossible for there to be 3.3 billion people simultaneously spending bitcoin in practice. It is not possible to confirm the transactions within any timescale that may be considered realistic.

The Taxation System For Crypto Currencies

The United States Internal Revenue Service (IRS) provided tax instructions regarding cryptocurrency in March of 2014. A comparatively small number of people have gone to the trouble of analyzing it. According to the Internal Revenue Service (IRS), all forms of virtual currency are to be regarded as properties rather than as currencies. Because of this proclamation, each stakeholder is responsible for understanding the intricate reporting obligations that are necessary.

Because of the outstanding performance of cryptocurrencies, particularly Bitcoins, the IRS has issued a ruling that is actually favorable for investors who have investments in virtual currencies. This ruling means that investors who have investments in virtual currencies will have to pay a lower tax rate because the gains and losses from their investments will be treated as capital gains, which are taxed at a rate that is lower than that of ordinary income. However, due to the nature of the short-term nature of their investments, active traders of digital currencies will be subject to taxation at the same rates as ordinary income.

The judgement issued by the IRS will have a significant impact on investors who have suffered losses as a result of their investments. They will have a difficult time writing off poor investments because the Internal Revenue Service places a limit of $3,000 annually on the amount of losses that can be claimed as tax returns. This will make it difficult for them to write off bad investments. Because of this, significant losses incurred through trading will not be able to be written off as "foreign currency" losses but will instead have to be carried over to subsequent years.

The concept of profiting from cryptocurrency investments is actually very straightforward. However, due to the fact that the true market value of virtual currencies might differ from one exchange to another, it may be difficult for many speculators to determine how much their investments would cost. Because these websites give their traders access to their transaction histories, conducting business with third-party exchanges can be made simpler. On the other hand, it can be more difficult for those who do business with local communities or merchants in their neighborhoods. The Internal Revenue Service (IRS) simply demands that the fair market value of the digital currency be reported at the day it was received, which is a huge relief for taxpayers.

Theoretically, the new cost basis of the buyer is the same as the investor's usage of the current fair market value while selling his digital currency. In actuality, there is not really any method to guarantee consistent reporting at all. There is a possibility that investors and traders will disclose contradicting costs because they may benefit financially from doing so.

It's possible that early investors and miners will be able to sidestep tax-reporting requirements because to the Internal Revenue Service's (IRS) hazy definition of what constitutes taxable virtual currencies. The Internal Revenue Service decided to adopt the definition provided by the Financial Crimes Enforcement Network. According to the definition, virtual currencies that are regarded to be taxable include those that can be converted into a real world currency.

If the cryptocurrency in question is listed on an exchange and there is an established exchange rate that is determined by supply and demand, then it is possible to exchange it for a traditional form of money. If they convert their convertible digital currencies to a digital currency with a lesser value, like Dogecoin, then wait for it to gain in value and trade on US exchanges, some traders and investors in virtual currencies may be able to avoid the requirement to file tax returns.

In addition, investors may use the digital currency to purchase a physical asset since the IRS has suggested, in a document that was made public, that a tax liability may be incurred if the convertible virtual currency is used to pay for goods and services in a real transaction. This suggests that investors may use the digital currency to purchase a physical asset.

Put Your Faith In Your Initial Thoughts.

When you look at a chart for the first time, you should be able to get a solid sense of the direction in which the price is trending. This is a principle that I believe in wholeheartedly. If you are unable to tell, this indicates that the chart is sending mixed signals, and you should go elsewhere for information that can provide you with a "read" that is more clear. How discriminating we are with our competition entries is a significant contributor to whether or not we make a profit. Keeping this in mind, you should look for a trade setup that is obvious to you the moment you lay eyes on it.

How can one develop that "gut feeling" or "muscle memory" to be able to recognize the difference between a good chart and a bad chart simply by looking at it? There are crucial components to any downtrend reversal, such as a higher low followed by a lower high break. These components have been explored in prior courses, so you should be familiar with them.

"The most lucrative business opportunities will appear out of nowhere and smack you in the face. When you have to concentrate more to find anything, there is a greater chance that you are trying to force the action.

You can see the growing power in a chart that has been putting in a string of higher lows and higher highs and is displaying strong volume on breakouts. This indicates that the strength is growing. Or, it's possible that you've seen that the price is approaching a significant level that has frequently acted as support in the market's history. It's possible that you'll conclude that this is an excellent opportunity for a trade with a limited stop loss.

In any case, with a sufficient amount of time and experience, you will eventually come to acquire a sense of what you are looking at, regardless of whether it is an uptrend, a downtrend, or just sideways chop.

"Gut instinct shouldn't be discounted. The trouble is, you can only get it through experience, and the best way to get that experience is to watch the chart for a number of hours every day.

Extremely Rare

The NFT marketplace known as SuperRare was first introduced in the year 2017. The platform is devoted to digital art, and it gives artists the ability to turn their work into NFTs so that it may be sold on the platform itself.

As a potential purchaser, all you need to do is choose an item from the collection of artwork that piques your interest. After that, you have the option to either pay the price listed for the item or make an offer by putting a bid. After successfully completing the purchase of the piece of art, you will have the option to either add it to your collection or to resell it on the secondary market to other people who also collect art. You have the option of displaying your art collection on the platform itself, or you can choose to do so in any digital gallery, virtual reality gallery, or any other location of your choosing.

In order to sell your digital artwork, you must first authenticate it, which requires you to digitally sign it and produce a tokenized certificate showing that you are the owner of the artwork. If you are an artist attempting to sell your digital artwork, you must authenticate it. After the authenticity of your work has been established, you will have the option to either sell it at a predetermined price or open it up for collectors to bid on it. However, as the service is still in its beta phase (also known as early access), they are only accepting a select few artists for the program at this time. In spite of this, you can still fill out a form in order to increase the likelihood of receiving an invitation to exhibit your artwork in the near future.

The Virtuous Earth

Terra Virtua is an immersive collectible video game that was released across many platforms in 2019. Users are able to exchange, trade, and engage with digital treasures in a way that is socially engaging and immersive since the platform provides a cohesive ecosystem that spans many platforms and is compatible with both augmented reality and virtual reality.

You can create your own personal art gallery and fill it with one-of-a-kind art collectibles that you've acquired from a variety of artists. Similarly, if you take use of the immersive features that are provided by the platform, you will be able to use your digital treasures in the same way that you would use real game things. Simply said, Terra Virtua gives you the ability to view and interact with your digital assets in a 3D environment using Augmented Reality and Virtual Reality online, via their mobile app, and in a 3D environment using their mobile app.

Kolect is the platform's very own native currency, and it can be purchased for $0.7607 per token at the moment. There are now 219,201,959 Kolect tokens in circulation, and the market value of all Kolect tokens combined is $167.14 million.

The Best of the NBA

The National Basketball Association (NBA) is supporting the non-fungible marketplace known as NBA Top Shot, which is called Non-Fungible. The year 2020 saw the birth of this site as a marketplace where anyone may buy and sell portions of NBA activity. The fundamental function of Top Shot is to transform exciting highlights into a form of digital collectibles known as moments. The buyer or owner of an NFT is awarded ownership over a certain instant in the game when that moment is converted into an action-packed highlight and sold as an NFT.

Because it has attracted more than 271,000 traders and produced an all-time trade volume of $449.37 million since its launch, the platform has effectively become the number one marketplace with the biggest number of users and trading volume. Since its launch, the platform has generated an all-time trade volume of $449.37 million. On the other hand, the site is only used for the sale of NBA moments, and original purchasers have the ability to resell their purchases on any secondary market.

Axie, the Infinite Axe

Axie Infinity is a blockchain-based game that is comparable to the breeding game CryptoKitties in terms of gameplay. The players get the opportunity to acquire magical beings called as Axies in this game. These non-playable characters are one of a kind and come equipped with special abilities that give them significant value in the game. Axies, like CryptoKitties cats, can be bred with one another to generate offspring that are distinct from other Axies and have features that are hard to find in other Axies. As a result of the fact that Axies may be used in the game to compete in battle tournaments, and the winner of such tournaments is awarded crypto rewards, Axies have a high value. Players are always on the lookout for Axies with rare attributes that perform well in battle and win, so they can utilize those Axies to increase their chances of success. In order to improve their gaming experience and increase their chances of winning a combat tournament, players are required to make strategic purchases of non-fungible token (NFT) game assets. As a direct consequence of this requirement, the demand for such NFTs is extremely strong on the platform.

Since its introduction in 2020, the digital collectibles platform known as Foundation has experienced remarkable expansion thanks to the efforts of its active user community. When the site first went live, it extended invitations to fifty artists, and those artists each received two further invites to give away to other prospective users of the platform.

The Atomic Market.

AtomicMarket is a one-of-a-kind marketplace designed specifically for NFTs, and it is incorporated into the AtomicAssets hub. Users of this NFT market have the ability to post NFTs for sale or put them up for auction on the market. Nevertheless, what makes this particular NFT market stand out from others is the fact that, in the role of a seller, you are granted the right to retain ownership of the NFT until a buyer is found for it. Permit me to elaborate a bit more.

When a seller wants to post their NFTs for sale on other NFT markets, they are required to also list their NFTs for sale on those marketplaces themselves. On the other hand, if you are using AtomicMarket to sell an NFT, you do not instantly have to transfer the funds to your account on the platform after posting the item for sale there. Instead, a trade offer function is used to post your NFT for sale on the platform, and the only time you will move the NFT to the platform will be when someone accepts your offer and acquires the asset. This indicates that you are free to list that particular NFT on other platforms or even carry on using it in dApps while you wait for someone to accept your trade offer on AtomicMarket.

Since the beginning of 2021, when the site was first made available to users, it has succeeded in luring 35,953 merchants to its marketplace and has produced $8.64 worth of total trading volume.

Over the past few years, there has been a steady rise in demand for non-fungible tokens (NFTs), which has resulted in the establishment of multiple NFT exchanges. When searching to purchase or sell NFTs, it is vital to evaluate the trading volume as well as the quantity of a marketplace before making a decision. There are undoubtedly a lot of promising NFT marketplaces on which you may trade NFTs. The greater the trading volume and the number of users of a certain marketplace, the greater the amount of liquidity that the marketplace has to provide. The following table provides a list of some NFT markets together with information regarding their trading volume and a number of users. You can use the list to figure out which marketplace has the most liquid assets to trade in so that you can carry out your NFT activities.

However, as a savvy investor, here is how to safeguard yourself; more specifically, how to invest in a revolution without suffering financial losses.

Keep your focus on the Core Currencies: Constructing your investment portfolio using the primary cryptocurrencies is the better course of action. These currencies are more likely to remain relevant in the market throughout the course of a longer period of time.

You might also diversify your holdings by purchasing a few utility tokens or minor currencies. However, you should be aware that in the event of a bubble bursting, these assets will most likely be the ones to take the initial and most severe damage.

Watch Out for Initial Coin Offerings: There are just too many projects entering the market at this time, and you need to be extremely careful to avoid participating in too many ICOs at the same time. Initial coin offerings (ICOs) are very appealing, and it's fair to not want to miss out on opportunities to earn a profit. However, there are just too many projects entering the market at this time.

Steer clear of leverage: If you are not a seasoned investor, you should steer clear of this at all costs. When trading, the use of leverage refers to the practice of employing borrowed funds or other financial instruments in the expectation of realizing enormous returns in the future.

Leverage trading should not be attempted on the cryptocurrency market while it is still in its infancy and subject to wild fluctuations.

Cash out Your Initial Investment: When you are in the deep profit zone, instead of being overly greedy, you should cash out your initial investment and start trading with the profits you have made.

Do not invest money that you do not fully want to lose or money that you have borrowed from someone else. This is the most important piece of advice. Be smart, be sensible, and most importantly, be patient. This will help you avoid the shiny object syndrome, which is when you chase after every new currency or invention that comes out in the market. Following that, we will go over some strategies for making money off of the bitcoin bubble.

The Blockchain technology.

The majority of cryptocurrencies rely on the blockchain as its central ledger. A public ledger or database that is replicated across multiple nodes in a network is known as a blockchain. The ledger stores a collection of records for every transaction that takes place using the cryptocurrency. These records are organized into what are called blocks, and they are recorded in the sequence of time that they occurred. As a result of the blocks' reliance on cryptographic validation to attach themselves to one another, the resulting chain of blocks is indestructible, giving rise to the term "blockchain." Each block includes a hashing function, a time stamp, and data about the transactions that contributed to the block. The hashing function makes a reference to the block that came before it. As a result, the blockchain is the repository of a record of each and every transaction that has ever taken place on the network ever since it was first established. As further blocks of transaction records are uploaded to the ledger, the size of the ledger continues to increase.

Due to the decentralized nature of the blockchain, there is no one authoritative copy of the ledger. Instead, a newly updated copy of the blockchain is sent to every computer that is part of the network. Everyone on the network is able to view the same list of transactions, which assures that the system is open and honest. Consensus is always present across the whole blockchain network, which is comprised of computers. Before a subsequent transaction can take place, each transaction must first be reconciled with all of the computers that are part of the network. After being included in the blockchain, blocks cannot be deleted or altered in any way. These records are secure and cannot be altered in any way. In order to tamper with a blockchain, an adversary would need to control all of the computers that are part of the network. Due to the decentralized and distributed structure of the blockchain, there is no central point at which it may potentially fail. Because of this, the security of cryptocurrencies is improved because there is no single point in the network that can be compromised.

There are nodes

Individual computers that are connected to the blockchain network are referred to as "nodes," and they form the basis of a blockchain network. Because these machines are running the blockchain protocol, they are able to communicate with the other nodes that are part of the network.

Within a blockchain network, nodes are responsible for the most crucial operation. On the network, "administrator" duties are shared among all of the nodes. It is entrusted with the responsibility of validating in an authoritative manner each and every transaction that takes place on the network. The nodes, having completed the validation of the transaction, subsequently record the transaction. The blockchain is updated whenever a new block is added to it by one of the nodes. These kinds of nodes may be referred to as fully validating nodes by certain blockchain networks. When a new computer is added to a blockchain network, it immediately receives a copy of the blockchain in the form of an automated download. Computers are able to join a blockchain on their own volition. Nodes have the opportunity to earn units of a cryptocurrency if they verify transactions and add them to blocks, which is the primary motivation for them to do so.

When a transaction takes place, the node examines the data associated with the transaction and independently confirms that the transaction is legitimate in every respect. It next checks to see if there is a potential that the coins have been spent twice, by comparing the transaction in question with its own version of the blockchain. In the event that a node receives a transaction that contains erroneous data, it will not only discard the transaction but will also terminate its contact with the node that sent it. Mistrust underpins the communication that takes place between individual nodes on a network. In the event that one node on the network transmits inaccurate transaction data to the others, the other nodes on the network will instantly isolate it. They sever all ties with it and remove it from the network entirely.

If the nodes come to the conclusion that a transaction is legitimate, then they will send it on to the miners (we will discuss this further in the following section). Miners collect the transactions and organize them into blocks in a sequential fashion before sending the blocks back to the nodes. The blocks are added to the blockchain as soon as the nodes concur that they should be considered legitimate. Nodes are responsible for verifying the correctness of blocks because they are unable to spread inaccurate information.

Since Bitcoin was the first cryptocurrency ever created, it is only fitting that we begin our journey there. Bitcoin is the progenitor of all other cryptocurrencies. When we talk about Bitcoin, we are going to go over several concepts that are fundamental to the majority of the other main currencies, if not all of them.

Bitcoin is a digital currency that was developed relatively recently in response to a pressing demand. Before the advent of Bitcoin, the most common way for people to trade currency with one another via the internet was to use reputable third-party intermediaries like PayPal, banks, or credit card companies like Visa and MasterCard. In the real world, the simplest way to transfer money is to pass cash directly to the recipient; there is no requirement for a middleman to be involved in this process. This is in contrast to a bank transfer, in which you put your faith in one or more third parties to conduct the transaction on your behalf in accordance with the terms and conditions that were previously agreed upon by the account holders, but which they rarely actually understand.

Bitcoin eliminates the need for these reliable third parties to participate in the transaction. In 2009, a white paper was published with the proposal of a completely new currency to be known as Bitcoin, which would be based on a new technology known as a "blockchain." The blockchain is a public, distributed ledger that is constantly updated and contains a record of all Bitcoin transactions. It takes the place of a third party in the process of transferring money by authenticating and recording transactions so that they can be viewed by everyone. The blockchain is not a financial institution. It is neither a company nor a national government. It is neither a person or an organisation, and there is not a single website or server that can be taken down or seized. It is nothing more than a ledger that is updated and maintained by a network of computers that are spread out over the entire world.

Take a few moments to digest what this information means to you. Bitcoin functions on the internet in a manner that is analogous to that of cash because there are no third parties involved. Because there are no payment processors, those who would normally be able to prohibit your transactions are unable to do so. Because you are your own bank, financial institutions and governments are unable to freeze your accounts.

It is also essential that you acknowledge the usefulness of the blockchain as a method of information recording and verification. This information could pertain to anything; it is not restricted to account balances or transactions involving money. The information that is maintained on the blockchain might be used to represent user accounts, deeds to property like as houses or automobiles, marriages, copyrights, licences, or anything else. In the case of Bitcoin, on the other hand, the blockchain serves as a public ledger that records all monetary transactions that take place on the Bitcoin network. How does one know for sure that the ledger they are using is accurate and trustworthy? The idea of consensus becomes relevant at this point in the discussion. The concept of consensus refers to when numerous computers check the ledger and come to an agreement as to which version is the most correct.

A blockchain is precisely what its name suggests it is: a chain of blocks, each of which contains data pertaining to a cryptocurrency transaction. The blocks are linked together or "stacked" in the order of time. In the case of Bitcoin, for instance, a single block can be broken down into numerous individual transaction records. The completion of a block and its subsequent verification by the network will result in its addition to the chain in an unalterable form. After that point, the contents of the block can no longer be altered without the consensus of the vast majority of the computers that are connected to the network.

"Miners" are specialised nodes on the Bitcoin network, and their mission is to ensure that the blockchain is kept up to date. Each miner, as well as each group (pool) of miners, is continuously focusing their attention on solving a particular mathematical issue. Not only is it challenging to find a solution to this issue, but the difficulty of doing so actually increases as more individuals look for a solution. The participant who is the first to correctly solve the challenge will be given the opportunity to add the next block of transactions to the blockchain. They are rewarded with newly produced bitcoin for their efforts, and in addition to this, they get to keep all of the transaction fees that were included in the block that they just wrote. The miner who is responsible for writing the block has the ability to choose which transactions are included in the block... and it is in that miner's best interest to choose the transactions that come with related transaction fees. Therefore, despite the fact that the transaction costs are theoretically optional, you should always include the proper fee if you want the miners to care enough about your transaction to confirm it, even though the transaction fees are legally optional. The vast majority of alternative cryptocurrencies follow a model that is analogous to bitcoin's, albeit with a few key changes, like the specific mathematical issue that must be solved, how the level of difficulty increases, how miners are compensated, and so on.

Additionally, Bitcoin was the first cryptocurrency to introduce the concept of digital wallets, which store the cryptocurrency at distinct addresses. These addresses are roughly comparable to account numbers at financial institutions. Even while this is a gross oversimplification, it is true enough for the majority of people to use Bitcoin without having an in-depth understanding of what is taking place behind the scenes in their wallet.

Bitcoin has been an enormously successful venture. Since it was first introduced in 2009, its value has exploded, going from less than one dollar to more over four thousand dollars in 2017. It is becoming widely accepted as a means of payment by businesses and financial organisations all over the world, and some investors now consider it as a store of value, much in the same way that gold or silver is. However, there have been a few obstacles to overcome. Bitcoin, and cryptocurrencies in general, exist in a legal limbo. Some nations have outright prohibited them, while others have severely restricted their usage or access to them. Because of the widespread misunderstanding that Bitcoin may be used to remain anonymous, hackers and other criminals have begun using it as a way of payment for illegal goods and services. Because to fraudulent activity, hacking, and other issues, a number of significant Bitcoin exchanges have been forced to close their doors or go out of business.

In spite of these obstacles, the use of Bitcoin and cryptocurrencies more generally has increased in popularity. Many users find the fact that these digital assets are decentralised to be particularly tempting because, for the most part, they are exempt from the laws and regulations that are applied to conventional currencies and other financial instruments. However, despite the fact that Bitcoin was the first and remains the most popular cryptocurrency, this does not necessarily mean that it is the best. There are a great number of other projects that have taken Bitcoin as their point of departure and developed beyond it. This book's goal is to examine a selection of the most notable achievements in recent history.

Bitcoin continues to be praised for its longevity, its steadiness, and its dependability despite the proliferation of new cryptocurrencies. Additionally, it is difficult to compete with Bitcoin's large market share; it continues to maintain its dominance of the marketplaces for cryptocurrencies.

The Market For Cryptocurrency

In this chapter, we will continue our exploration of cryptocurrency trading as well as discuss the cryptocurrency market.

Trade in Cryptocurrencies

There are two different ways to begin active trading in a trade. Because of the favourable cost structure of one of the options, it is recommended that you begin trading with this one, particularly if you are just starting out. The second choice is more accurate and offers more professional advantages, but it comes at a significantly higher price. Making a decision is never simple.

When you are just starting out, it might be tough to decide which option is best for you. There are numerous things to think about, but when you are first getting started, the most important thing is to select the option that will be least expensive for you, presuming that you intend to take things gently at first. Going online wouldn't be a problem for you if this is your first time participating in the cryptocurrency market; let's suppose you start out with between 5 and 10 Bitcoin. When you start with that amount, you will most likely engage in between three and five trades each day. At this juncture, the online transaction shouldn't present any problems.

Trading houses and online exchanges will give you the opportunity to carry out trades and give you access to trading tools that you can use to hunt for buy and sell points in the market. This service is provided for free by a number of different intermediaries, provided that you place a certain minimum amount with them.

You also have the choice of avoiding the usage of online trading platforms altogether and instead obtaining the price feed via the Bloomberg Terminal. Bloomberg provides real-time price quotes for the most important cryptocurrencies, including the vast majority of the more recent ones. They may also give you the ability to chart all of the cryptocurrencies and give you the flexibility to directly programme your approach based on your feed.

You should make an investment in the equipment that you are going to utilise if you are thinking about getting involved in crypto trading on a long-term basis. It is essential that you educate yourself on all of your available choices and potential costs.

If you end up deciding to execute rapid-fire trades and use the online system, you will need to ensure that you have a solid internet provider. Lag time is unacceptable for any degree of trading, so you will need to make sure that you have a stable internet connection.

Methods of Business Conduct

When you first start out trading cryptocurrencies, we are going to provide you with three different trading techniques that you can implement. These three trading approaches will serve as the basis for further trading approaches that you will become familiar with as a novice in order to enable you to develop and enhance your trading skills.

You need to keep in mind that the market is continuously moving in some direction since people are continually buying and selling things on it. This has the potential to become a full-time profession given that there are over 50 conceivable currency and fiat currency combinations.

Purchase the Dips.

A price movement that first marches forward and then takes a momentary step back is referred to as a "dip," and the term "dip" is used to characterise those times. The majority of markets are moving in this direction. There is a lot of quick movement. It is an efficient method to use when you are new to any kind of trading market and you are trying to discover patterns.

A trend can last anywhere from a few days to several months for traders who focus on the long term. They will take their place in their position, where they will remain for a few days, weeks, or months. On the other hand, a crypto day trader or a crypto scalper would never do something like that. A day trader is someone who aggressively "ride the waves," meaning they trade both up and down, and then departs the market within a matter of minutes or hours.

If you have opted to engage in rapid trades, seeing dips in the market will provide you with a better entry position at the beginning of a mini-rally. This will serve as your primary plan to begin with.

Immediately after starting, look at the graphical representation of the changes in price. It is not necessary for you to worry too much about the numbers; they are not significant. Those figures are not capable of providing you with an accurate representation of the price as it starts to take shape. Observe the chart and, in order to gain a sense of the dynamics of the movement, alter the timeline such that it first shows 5 seconds, then 10 seconds, and finally 1 minute. Take note of how each new high point is followed by a new low point, and how each new low point is followed by a surprising new high point. You are going to have to grow accustomed to this kind of pattern in order to successfully buy the dip.

You should never place an order at the same moment that the market begins to move in the opposite direction of the trend it has been following. You should wait for the price to drop before purchasing it on the next run it makes. If you do this, you won't have to face the retracements as soon as you enter the arena; instead, you'll be able to see the rally form. In addition, this enables you to validate the movement forward. You can use falling prices as a signal to enter the market at the appropriate time.

When you are sorting the market, it is also important for you to wait for the dip. At this juncture, the dip takes on an entirely new significance; it is pulling back from its downward trend and momentarily climbing higher. Take things slowly and carefully.

Attend its arrival. The moment it reaches its peak and starts to head back down is the right time to seize the opportunity. You should never even attempt to capture it at its highest point. Although it will guarantee you a perfect catch at the same moment the price is at its highest, in the long run, it will not be as good.

Both the apex and the pit serve a distinct function, and that function is not to enable you to harvest or liquidate resources; rather, it is to enable you to plan out your future course of action. Your trigger points should be located at the top and bottom of the curve.

Bitcoin: Some Interesting Facts

Bitcoin is now the most widely used form of virtual currency, and it has steadily been gaining both popularity and power over the course of the past year. At first glance, Bitcoin may appear to be confusing; nevertheless, the following are a few Bitcoin fun facts that can help clear things up for you.

The cryptocurrency known as bitcoin is an open-source software, which means that it is not controlled by a single body and that anyone and everyone can use it. The exact same manner that you can connect to a website and download some pictures or songs is the exact same method that you can get Bitcoin. In addition, there is no company that stood behind the development of Bitcoin; nonetheless, since the originator of Bitcoin is unknown, there is no owner.

There is a limited amount of Bitcoins available.

As was discussed before, there is a finite amount of Bitcoins in circulation, which is one of the primary reasons why the currency is considered to be stable and why it carries a particular value. In the same way that other materials and substances have incredible value due to their rarity and limited quantity, bitcoins have the same quality. Everything that is restricted on earth has a magnificent value.

Bitcoins do not have an innate or predetermined value.

This is just another reason why Bitcoin retains its singular and unprecedented value. There is no other form of currency or anything else that Bitcoin could have inherited its value from. Bitcoin has a value, but that value might change depending on the services that have been performed in exchange for it.

You are able to observe every single transaction.

Because it is software that is freely available to everyone, all information pertaining to bitcoin, including a detailed report of the transactions, is also freely available. Because there is no single individual behind the currency, the information about it is not under the control of anyone in particular. You can do a quick search on the internet to find all the specific information you need regarding Bitcoin transactions, and you can be certain that you will locate the information that you require.

You can "mine" Bitcoin As was mentioned before, there are several ways for you to obtain bitcoin, and one of the most effective ways is referred to as "mining." You may "mine" bitcoin by using the address of a Bitcoin wallet. People that earn Bitcoin by solving math problems while utilising specialised software that will distribute a set amount of Bitcoin in exchange for those solutions are referred to as "math miners." This word is used to describe those people. The individuals who are responsible for this kind of work are referred to as "miners." This is one of the most interesting ways to design a currency, and it motivates individuals to deal with mathematical problems. It is also one of the most interesting ways to construct a money.

It is not possible to undo a transaction in order to avoid having to pay.

There is no way to reverse a transaction that has already been completed using Bitcoin. In other words, a transaction cannot be reversed after it has already taken place. Because you will be required to use a website that appropriately handles operations, you can have faith in the level of security they provide. You also don't need to worry about being forced to pay for something simply because it's a digital currency; it's the same as regular money, so there's no need for anxiety there. You are not required to make a payment for anything if you do not like to do so.

It is possible for you to "end money with little to no fee."

When you send money to someone else using Bitcoin, there are no fees since there is no one owner of Bitcoin. Since there is no single owner of Bitcoin, there is also no single person or entity that can earn a profit off of the transactions.

Bitcoins are kept in digital wallets at this time.

If you were wondering where you would store your Bitcoins, the answer is simple: you would have a wallet, but it will be digital. If you were wondering where you would keep your Bitcoins, the answer is simple. It is the same thing as a bank account, with the exception that it has a different name; in addition, you will not be required to pay any annual or monthly fees in order to maintain that wallet. It functions as a physical wallet, and once you have all of your Bitcoins gathered in one location, you will be able to do virtually anything you want with them.

Keeping those bitcoins in your wallet means you won't have to worry about losing them.

The most perilous aspect of the baccarat is that you will not be able to retrieve your winnings until the other player has satisfied your debt. Because of this, you should take precautions to ensure the safety of your Bitcoin wallet and conduct business only with reputable vendors. Be very careful when storing your money and when spending it, as if you were to lose your wallet, you would be in a position where you could not get your money back in any way.

Bitcoin can be used to pay for a wide variety of goods and services.

You will be able to purchase anything so long as the vendor of the good accepts payment in bitcoin. If they do, then you will have no problem making your purchase. This is becoming increasingly popular, and as a result, you will find an increasing number of things at your disposal that can be purchased with Bitcoin. As stated above, there are more than 100 firms accepting Bitcoin worldwide.

You can have anonymity

This is one of the best perks of Bitcoin; there is no trace back to you, and that is the main reason why more countries are banning and prohibiting the use of this currency. You can pay for anything with Bitcoin and remain completely anonymous.

The Difference Between Fungible And Non-Fungible Assets

It is vital to get an understanding of (or refresh one's memory on) the concepts of assets, tokens, tokenization, and Blockchain in order to get a better grasp on the distinction between fungible and non-fungible.

What exactly is an asset?

The term "asset" comes from the world of finance and denotes anything that has been given a monetary value and has the potential to be useful or desired. It may be a tangible object, a digital representation, an abstract concept, or anything else that helps produce earnings. Because it has the same value as other assets, a fungible asset can be exchanged for any other fungible item. Bitcoin, for instance, qualifies as a fungible asset due to the fact that one bitcoin is equivalent in value to any other bitcoin. Fungibility is a desirable quality in a currency because it enables free exchange even when there is no way to determine the history of each unit. This makes fungibility an attractive feature. However, the trait of fungibility does not contribute to the value of collectibles.

Something that cannot be exchanged for something else or even divided up into smaller parts is referred to as a non-fungible asset. For instance, a house, a used automobile, or a one-of-a-kind football card are all examples of non-fungible investments. This cannot be divided into two parts since each part would have a different value. A token is nothing more than the digital representation of something, and that something can be anything so long as it has features that are recognized and certifiable.

A token is a digital representation of value that is used in the context of the blockchain technology. Tokens are typically issued by companies. Tokens are units of value that represent a digital asset (such as a cryptocurrency, a physical commodity or thing, etc.). Tokens can be used in a variety of applications.

A token, in its broadest sense, is an object that possesses a certain value solely within the confines of a given context.

Could you give me an example? Chips from the casino. These chips are nothing more than bits of plastic with no value outside the four walls of the casino. Within this framework, their value is determined, and they are subsequently transformed into the representation of an asset.

Throughout history, tokens have been used to generate currency that have value within a certain context. Therefore, the worth of a token is determined by the decision that its creator makes regarding how much value to give it.

Tokenization refers to the process that takes place within the context of blockchain technology when a particular property and value are allocated to a token. The Blockchain is a type of distributed ledger technology that can be compared to a database in that it gathers confidential information from many computer systems and online networks.

Decentralization, transparency, and immutability are the three fundamental principles that underpin blockchain technology. Blockchain technology makes it possible to operate in a decentralized paradigm, in which no single computer is in charge of the entire network. A decentralized system makes it possible for there to be more transparency: every action that takes place within the Blockchain is recorded, and anybody can keep the log of activities and transactions updated. It is extremely difficult to discover a model that accurately represents the physical world that has such a high level of transparency, in which everything is recorded and can be viewed by everyone. Additionally, this data cannot be altered in any way, and as a result, it is said to be immutable.

A non-fungible token (NFT) is the one-of-a-kind representation of a natural or digital asset that cannot be traded for an equivalent since there is no equal asset. An NFT can be created when a digital asset is tokenized using blockchain technology. There is no other NFT anywhere in the world that can be compared to it. There no limit to what individuals can achieve with NFTs. The potential for applications include a wide variety of domains, including but not limited to the arts, online gaming, music, collectibles of varying kinds, rare luxury goods, virtual properties, and many other areas. People are given ownership and administration of the token, as well as the option to transfer it to a platform that is decentralized, transparent, and unchangeable thanks to blockchain technology, which gives digital assets certain features not seen in traditional assets.

The Buy-And-Hold Investment Strategy's Many Benefits In A Rising Market

1. Eliminates 95% of the noise in the market

The long-term bull trend line serves to strengthen the buy and hold trading strategy by reducing the noise in the market that is caused by a lower trading period. Trading patterns over short time frames are typically unpredictable, which might have an impact on trades. For a given amount of time, the line on a weekly chart depicting price actions will not be volatile.

2. Decreased amounts spent on transactions

Traders that focus on the long term and use the buy-and-hold strategy do not engage in excessive trading. The transaction expenses can be greatly reduced with this method. A short-term trader who engages in weekly or daily trades, on the other hand, is required to take into account the accumulated transaction costs associated with each trade individually.

When compared to the execution of a few long-term trades, trading on multiple short-term trades will result in significantly higher costs.

3. Lessens the effects of stress on the mind

Especially for less experienced traders, the execution of multiple deals with short-term or medium-term time horizons can be an extremely stressful experience. The buy-and-hold strategy causes significantly less anxiety than more frequent trading. The buy-and-hold technique is significantly less stressful than short selling, despite the fact that it can still be difficult at times.

4. It is not vital to have perfect timing in the market

Because it does not involve any market time, the buy-and-hold investment approach is appealing to a lot of different traders. Traders are able to enter the market without having to be on the lookout for a significant drop in the direction of an approaching bull market trend. Long-term investors are aware that if they rely on perfect market timing, they run the risk of missing out on prospective opportunities.

5. Effective use of time

The buy-and-hold trading approach is perfect for investors who want to maximize their profits while minimizing the amount of time they spend trading. Long-term investors do not need to constantly monitor price changes on a daily basis or utilize charts based on technical analysis to keep an eye on price fluctuations. In spite of this, they should never stop monitoring the basic news pertaining to the cryptocurrency market and should check their position at regular intervals so that they can profit from their investment in crypto-assets.

6. Reduced tax rates

Capital gains can be substantial for crypto assets that are held for extended periods of time. Investments that have been held for at least a year before being sold can qualify for reduced tax rates. Long-term tax rates, rather than the higher short-term tax rates, are applicable to the assets.

7. The cost in dollars An average of

An investor who uses the Buy and Hold strategy will often invest on a consistent timetable, such as once per week or once per month. Many investors make monthly purchases of $100 worth of bitcoin. The result is averaged out as the price fluctuates both up and down. If the trend over the long term is a bull market, the investor can expect to see an increase in the value of their assets.

What Are The Benefits, In General, Of Purchasing Cryptocurrency Or Making An Investment In It?

If you have been paying attention and following along with the first two chapters, you should now be familiar with the underlying ideas that underpin cryptocurrencies. A few of the issues that are going to be discussed below have been touched on briefly before. Nevertheless, despite the fact that they are equally significant, each one deserves to be highlighted in this context.

Before reading about the individual sets of advantages and disadvantages for Bitcoin, Litecoin, and Ethereum, it is important to first discuss the benefits that are inherent to cryptocurrencies in general. When you get to the more currency-specific lists, keep these in mind as you go through them.

1. The use of a 'Pseudonym'

One of the most common misunderstandings concerning Bitcoin and alternative cryptocurrencies is the idea that anyone who uses them will instantly become anonymous to the individuals with whom they transact business. However, not all of that is accurate. Because there is no way to conduct a transaction with bitcoins without leaving some trace of your identity behind, the fundamental concept of anonymity is undermined. This is evidenced by the fact that every wallet possesses its own one-of-a-kind address. That, by itself, already gives people certain fundamental identifiers that they can utilize.

However, there is a phrase that more accurately describes the private nature of utilizing digital currency, and that term is "pseudonymity." Every person's wallet has its own unique code, often known as its "pseudonym." This situation is very similar to the one that typically takes place in online forums, in which participants are familiar with one another's identities based on their usernames. Aside from the one topic that acts as the impetus for why they are participating in the same discussion forum at the same time, they don't really know very much about each other's private lives. In spite of everything, they will still be able to accomplish the purpose for which they came, which is to discuss topics of interest to them in common.

Now, let's talk about why this is seen as a benefit. The level of anonymity that may be achieved through the use of cryptocurrencies cannot be replicated by any other sort of monetary transaction. This is something that has not changed. When one chooses the former, there is no possibility that their personal information or credit card details will be stolen. The only possible exception to this rule would be if someone were to publicly disclose all of their wallet addresses. But can you think of anyone else in the world who would act in such a way?

2. Unchangeability

The impossibility of making changes to transactions that have already been validated is one of the most distinctive features of the blockchain technology. To refresh your memory, a blockchain functions similarly to a ledger in that it is shared with all members of the network who have ever taken part in any activity that is relevant. Blockchain technology can be used in a variety of applications, but you should focus your attention first on its role as the essential component of cryptocurrencies. As a result, the reason for its immutability will be explained in relation to that situation.

Take, for example, the procedure of mining once more. A miner that has successfully extracted a block from the blockchain would have validated a specific transaction; for the sake of this example, we will refer to this transaction as Trans A. Consider the scenario in which someone wants to replace Trans A with Trans B. That person would need to do a new mining operation on the block that contains that transaction and figure out the solution to the computational issue that would verify Trans B instead. In order to ensure that there are no inconsistencies, it is necessary for him to carry out this procedure once more for each block that comes after the initial block that Trans A created. Aside from all of that, he would also need to make sure that all of his changes are reflected on each and every copy of the blockchain. This is in addition to everything else. The entirety of the process is not simple, which is why you might validate that transactions with Bitcoin are comparable to getting a tattoo on your face — once it's there, no one can claim that it isn't there. This is because once it's there, no one can say that it isn't there.

In this context, the quality of being immutable is advantageous since, to reiterate, it prevents illegal activities such as the falsification of documents. Additionally, this feature comes bundled with another one called "permanence," which ensures that your transactional records will survive your death and can be used as a reference by your next of kin after you're gone.

3. The Simplicity of Business Deals

If you utilize cryptocurrencies instead of fiat currency, then all of your transactions will take place online. This means that the inherent ease of the internet will apply to all of your non-fiat financial dealings. In terms of the expenses associated with currency exchange, well, there won't be any; or at the very least, these will be quite modest. One last thing to consider is the breadth of feasible commercial alliances. Your trading partner could be anybody from anywhere in the world so long as they have the necessary tools. If everything could be achieved without leaving the convenience of your own house and with the dependability of your own computer, you would not have to go through the inconvenience and expense of traveling to another country.

Maintain a flexible frame of mind as you read the responses to the questions that follow. Two of the benefits described above can, in some circumstances, also be seen as drawbacks.

Litecoin

Litecoin, often known as LTC, has been available for purchase on the market for two years as of today. The global financial markets are the target audience for this cryptocurrency. People feel that Litecoin (LTC) is similar to Bitcoin in some form or another. The majority of researchers are of the opinion that its inception was motivated by the success of Bitcoin. Charles Lee, the idealist, desires for Litecoin to provide services that are superior to those offered by Bitcoin. Because of this, Litecoin can be seen as an alternative to Bitcoin. The most prominent media outlets around the world have begun to view Litecoin as a potential competitor to Bitcoin.

Many publications, including The New York Times, have the opinion that it is more than just an alternative to Bitcoin. And according to the statistics of the market and its share, Litecoin is in second place. Those who are interested in utilizing Litecoin will utilize the most recent version. This version was made available to the public in April of this year. The 0.8.5.7 Version offers a great number of benefits. Transaction fees have been reduced in order to entice a large number of users. The version that is currently available also features improved security. There are three key differences between Litecoins and other cryptocurrencies. Among these are the following: - The interval at which blocks containing Litecoin are processed has been lowered to every two and a half minutes. This makes it superior to the Bitcoin transaction, which takes ten minutes, and also makes it faster. However, an increasing number of chained blocks makes it necessary to avoid other blocks. The vast majority of them are going to be neglected.

Litecoin is currently in first place due of the security protocol that it employs. Litecoin plans to compete directly with scrypts. Bitcoin makes use of additional formats in addition to scrypts, although these alternatives are not superior. The security protocol used is SHA-256.

- Each year, there will be a total supply increase of eighty four million Litecoins. This goes above and beyond the goal for Bitcoin. There will be four times as many Litecoins produced as there are Bitcoins available for purchase.

Ledgers are used in the process of conducting online transactions for Litecoin as well. It is possible for users to keep a record of the sums they have transacted. Servers are utilized in the maintenance of a secure environment as another function. The various wallets that have been made available to businessmen can be accessed by these individuals. There are several that are compatible with both Windows and MAC operating systems.

This year witnessed the launch of Google's digital wallet service for Android devices.

These currencies can be traded for a variety of other currencies via a variety of methods. It's possible that they'll be somewhere between Bitcoin and Litecoin. Dollars, Euros, and Yuan are some of the other currencies that are commonly used. It is possible to pay for various online services with Litecoins. The majority of them involve making purchases via the internet.

Mining, Bitcoin, And Other Cryptocurrencies

Bitcoin was the first cryptocurrency ever created, and it continues to maintain its position as the most widely used digital asset overall in the crypto market. The term "alternative currency to Bitcoin" (sometimes written as "Altcoins") refers to all cryptocurrencies that are not Bitcoin.

Bitcoin and the functionalities it possesses

Bitcoin, also known as "virtual gold," is a decentralized kind of digital currency that operates through the utilization of blockchain technology. Because the transaction takes place directly between the sender and the recipient on the basis of the peer to peer electronic cash transfer system – the blockchain technology – this virtual coin can be stored in a coin wallet (online or offline) and can serve as an exchange medium for transactions without the necessity of a third-party intervention (banks, financial bodies, etc.). This is because the transaction takes place based on the blockchain technology.

By ensuring that the distributed public ledger is always up to date, the blockchain in the Bitcoin network is responsible for keeping a record of all of the Bitcoin transactions that have ever taken place within the network. When a new request is made for a Bitcoin transaction, the previous transaction is examined to see whether or not it was genuine. The digital signatures contained within the transaction block ensure that the data is valid. Bitcoin miners are responsible for verifying transactions and, if they are successful, they are rewarded with cryptocurrency. Bitcoin is denoted by the ticker symbol BTC.

What is its purpose, exactly?

It is necessary to have a Bitcoin wallet pre-installed on your computer before you may participate in any Bitcoin transactions. After a successful installation, you will be able to create your first Bitcoin address, and you can then provide this address to your friends so that you can start conducting payments with them. A Bitcoin address can only ever be used once; in other words, a Bitcoin address can only ever be used to complete a single transaction. A brand-new Bitcoin address will need to be generated for each and every transaction that takes place. After each transaction is validated, a new block is added to the blockchain that the Bitcoin network uses.

The movement of currency that takes place between Bitcoin wallets is referred to as a Bitcoin transaction, and the data representing this value is added to the blockchain as part of the transaction. Along with the value, the transaction block will also include a private key (which can be located in the Bitcoin wallet) and a digital signature (which will help prevent a breach in security). This private key, which is also referred to as the seed, is used to sign transactions using a mathematical proof (hash), which is solved by the miner during the process of mining. This key is used to sign transactions using a mathematical proof. This hash verifies that the information was, in fact, transmitted by the owner of the Bitcoin.

When a Bitcoin transaction is started, the details of that transaction are immediately broadcast across the network. The miner then confirms the transaction within the following 10 minutes.

How do you actually use Bitcoin?

If a particular seller allows Bitcoin to be used as a form of payment for online transactions, then the digital currency can function similarly to traditional currencies in that it can be used to buy and sell goods and services online. You can do this if you want to buy an online game from a shopping website that allows Bitcoin as one of the payment mechanisms, and here is how the process works (behind the scenes):

In order for the transaction to be successful, the following information will be required.

- A string of numbers or letters that only you have access to (This string of private data will hold the specifics of your digital wallet address, the amount, and the transaction data.)

- The address of the recipient (which will include a publicly viewable sequence of letters and digits)

The merchant will decode the private key, and at this point, the other users on the Bitcoin network will receive the broadcast of the transaction request they have been waiting for. The miners will then confirm the transaction request within the next ten minutes, at which point the Bitcoin payment will be sent to the vendor.

Alternative coins

Because of the restrictions placed on Bitcoin transactions, new cryptocurrencies came into being. These new cryptocurrencies were referred to as Altcoins, which is short for "alternatives to Bitcoins." If you take a look at the bulk of the alternative cryptocurrencies that are currently available for purchase, you'll notice that they all provide completely unique characteristics that the original coin was unable to provide. For example, the 'smart contracts' technology that is supplied by the Ethereum platform, the altcoin known as 'IOTA' that functions as a machine-economy token, the altcoin known as 'Ripple' that allows inter-bank payments via blockchain, etc. are a few examples of this type of technology.

Before you decide to buy or trade using these new cryptocurrencies, it is important to study the 'white papers' of the individual altcoins on their official websites. These 'white papers' may be found on the websites of the different altcoins. Whether they are investors or traders, the vast majority of participants in the bitcoin market have one primary objective: to profit from their activities. When measured against Bitcoin's growth, altcoins are outpacing Bitcoin's performance in terms of percentage increases.

Before you can begin utilizing Altcoins for transactions, you will first need to store them in a coin wallet, just like you would do with Bitcoins. The following are the alternative cryptocurrencies that are utilized the most frequently: ether, litecoin, ripple, monero, bytecoin, iota, and dash and zcash

Working in mines The procedure

Mining is the procedure that helps generate or manufacture cryptocurrencies, and there is no other way to create these digital currencies besides this process. Mining is the only way to generate or make cryptocurrencies. 'Fiat currency' is produced when a government gives permission to a regulatory agency to print its respective currency based on the demand of the country's economy; this is the method by which 'fiat currency' is created. But in the case of cryptocurrencies, their generation will be restricted to the use of computers running specialized software in order to solve the associated cryptographic riddles. Mining is the process being described, and the individuals who participate in mining are referred to as miners.

How exactly does it function?

This transaction block is comprised of the transaction data, the hash, and the nonce. The new transaction block is suggested after all of the new requests are collected together into a block.

- The hash of the block is calculated in order to determine whether or not the value is lower than the target value, which is the specified hash value.

- The proof of work (PoW) problem is considered to have been solved when the value of the hash is less than the target value.

-      In the event that this is not the case, the nonce is advanced before the hash is recalculated.

The newly generated hash is examined once more to see whether or not it is lower than the predetermined value.

The procedure will be repeated over and over again until the PoW (proof of work) puzzle is resolved.

- The miner is rewarded in the form of crypto tokens (Bitcoin if it is Bitcoin mining, Ether if it is Ethereum mining, etc.) once the PoW (proof of work) has been solved.

The difficulty of mining resides in establishing the target hash value, which is intentionally meant to be tough so that there is a consistent rate of mining the transaction blocks. The Proof of Work protocol is an essential component in guaranteeing that each transaction block is validated and added to the blockchain in a timely manner.

The Workings Behind Virtual Currencies

In order to get a grasp on cryptocurrencies, it is essential that you have a firm grasp of the following fundamental ideas and words, which you will encounter frequently:

1. openly accessible ledgers

From the moment a cryptocurrency was founded, they have a record of all transactions that have been confirmed by various participating computers (nodes). Anyone who possesses the appropriate software to access it can view the information contained in this ledger. On the other hand, the identity of persons who hold different coins are hidden by ciphers. In point of fact, the system makes use of sophisticated cryptographic procedures in order to guarantee the authenticity and integrity of record keeping. The public ledger is often responsible for ensuring that linked digital wallets are able to accurately determine the amount of a coin owner's holdings that can be spent at any given time. Not only that, but whenever there is a new transaction, the system checks the records to make sure that each transaction uses coins that a particular spender truly holds in his or her account. This happens whenever there is a new transaction. The public ledger used by Bitcoin, for example, is referred to as a "transaction block chain."

2. Wallets in the Digital Age

As I mentioned earlier, cryptocurrencies are digital currencies that exist just in the virtual world; they do not exist in a physical form. This pretty much indicates that you require some location where you are able to access them if you do have any. A "digital wallet" is the name given to this particular location.

This essentially means that digital wallets are where you store your cryptocurrency holdings within a blockchain in a secure and private manner. In addition, you can utilize your wallet to transfer or receive whatever cryptocurrency you choose to use. Although each cryptocurrency has its own official wallet, the most of them also recommend a select few wallets developed by third parties.

These wallets can be downloaded from the cryptocurrency's official website.

The explanation presented above, however, is an oversimplification of the situation because, in point of fact, cryptocurrency assets are not really kept in a wallet. Your access to a private key, which is a secret digital code that is only known to you and the wallet itself, is the primary benefit of using a cryptocurrency wallet. The purpose of a private key is to provide evidence that an individual genuinely possesses a particular public key. A public key is a secure digital code that is associated with a specified quantity of a given currency. To put it another way, your digital wallet normally holds both your public and private keys. It also enables you to receive and transmit coins, and it serves as your own access point for the public ledger (you may think of it as your own personal record of the transactions involving bitcoin).

Which wallets, then, are the best choices for safely storing your cryptocurrency?

As I've already mentioned, each cryptocurrency has its own official wallet in addition to certain wallets that are recommended by third parties. For instance, there is a Bitcoin Core Wallet for Bitcoin, an Ethereum Wallet or MyEtherWallet for Ethereum, and a Litecoin-QT wallet for Litecoin. All of these wallets are available for download.

You can also make use of something that is known as a "universal wallet," such as HolyTransaction, which allows you to store a number of different cryptocurrencies.

For storage over a longer period of time, you might use offline wallets like TREZOR if you so choose.

Note: As a general guideline, you should never download any wallets from any source other than the official website.

I would recommend that you also sign up on an Exchange such as Coinbase, Kraken, or Coinmama since they will enable you to sell your cryptocurrency or buy new coins whenever you need to. Given that you will be wanting to trade in numerous cryptocurrencies, this is a recommendation that comes highly recommended.

3: Dealings and Exchanges

A transaction is any transfer of digital assets that takes place between two digital wallets. When you send some cryptocurrency, the client for your wallet generates a single data structure that uses an encrypted electronic signature. This happens whenever you send cryptocurrency. After that, the transaction is broadcasted via the network using the public ledger, which makes a mathematical evidence that such a transaction truly took place available to anyone who wants to see it. It is the responsibility of the cryptocurrency nodes on the network to relay the information of the transaction that has been broadcast, and once the legitimacy of the transaction has been verified, the nodes will include the transaction in the new block that they are mining.

4. The Nodes

In the context of any particular cryptocurrency network, this refers to a point of intersection or link. A machine that is taking part in the global cryptocurrency network can be considered a node. The computer takes part in the transaction by utilizing a cryptocurrency protocol, which enables communication to take place amongst the many nodes that make up the network. Their primary responsibility is to primarily propagate newly created blocks and transactions. Each node, which is a participating computer, obtains the data on the new transaction and independently checks every aspect of it. Then, it compares the data with a copy of the ledger that it was given in order to determine whether or not the amount that was spent is accurate. The moment that a node receives data that is invalid, it immediately rejects it and terminates communication with the user. Any node that makes an attempt to transmit an invalid transaction is immediately kicked off the network and barred from further participation in it. These nodes do not trust one another and waste no time in distancing themselves from any suspicious node that attempts to destroy the results of any transaction. They also do not share information with one another.

5. Encoding/Decoding

The process of transforming data or information into codes with the sole purpose of limiting unwanted access is referred to as data or information encoding. When you utilize cryptocurrencies as a medium of exchange, you will need two keys: one for encryption, and one for decryption. You cannot use the same key for both tasks. These keys are connected to one another through various mathematical operations. The encryption key is also known as the public key or the address that people must use in order to transfer payments to you. The other key, known as the private key or the password, is what you will need in order to decrypt the information. The public key is the address of the wallet, which may be used to transfer bits of data to other people, such as Bitcoins or any other type of coin, and through which other people can send you similar data. After such data has been encrypted, the only person who has access to the private key is you, therefore no one else can decrypt the content of any transaction without your help.

Mining (No. 6)

Mining, in its most fundamental sense, simply refers to the process by which nodes typically confirm transactions and then add them to the public ledger of a particular cryptocurrency. Mining may also be thought of as the act of creating new coin. In order for a node to add a transaction to the distributed ledger, it must first solve a demanding computational task that is getting progressively more challenging. Because mining is an open-source operation, which basically implies that every node can confirm any given transaction, there is no limit to the number of times a transaction can be confirmed. The person who is the first to figure out how to solve a riddle will be given the opportunity to add a new section of transactions to the ledger. The way the public blockchain ledger, blocks, and transactions function together creates an environment in which it is extremely difficult for anyone to arbitrarily edit or add any block. Having said that, any information (transactions) that are associated with a block once it has been put to the ledger are permanent. The miner who is responsible for adding a block to the blockchain is eligible for a reward consisting of some coins upon the successful addition of the block to the blockchain. In addition, a little transaction fee is applied.

In a method known as the proof of work, miners are given currencies as a reward for mining, which involves solving puzzles and adding a block that has been solved to the blockchain. This is important information for you to know.

7: Proof of Work In the world of cryptocurrency, the term "proof of work" refers to a method that employs functions that are difficult to compute but relatively simple to verify in an effort to limit the amount of profit that can be made from mining cryptocurrencies. Bitcoin mining almost exclusively makes use of the proof-of-work system. When people are mining digital currency and adding blocks of transactions to provided public ledgers, this effectively implies that what they are doing is really 'cracking' the proof of work system with the use of a variety of high powered computers in order to solve a certain mathematical problem. This is done in order to earn new digital money.

The 'Internet of Value' is something that Ripple wants to build. RippleNet, the company's payment network, provides links to hundreds of financial institutions around the world through the use of a single application programming interface (API). These connections allow for the transfer of funds to be completed in a more timely, affordable, and dependable manner. Ripple hopes that by doing so, it will be able to make the transfer of money throughout the world quicker, less expensive, and friendlier to the environment. We are now able to communicate information in a matter of seconds across a variety of platforms thanks to the internet. Ripple intends to accomplish the same thing with regard to money. It is the first blockchain in the entire network that collaborates with rather than competes with centralized financial institutions like banks and governments. These institutions include any organization that handles large amounts of money. At the moment, more than 300 of these kinds of institutions use the company's network, which is called RippleNet, to process payments made by customers. American Express, SBI Remit, and

MoneyGram are some of the options available.

Similar to other digital assets, XRP operates on the XRP Ledger, which serves as the cryptocurrency's own blockchain. It was established in 2012 with the primary purpose of reducing the amount of time spent processing payments. This ledger is capable of processing transactions in three to five seconds. In contrast to other cryptocurrencies, such as Bitcoin, which has a transaction fee of 0.50 dollars, the cost of one transaction in this cryptocurrency is 0.0002 dollars. This results in a significant reduction in cost. XRP can be sent directly to a recipient without passing via an intermediary, and it can be used for a wide variety of purposes, from microtransactions to international payments. Jed McCaleb, Arthur Britto, and David Schwartz are responsible for the development of XRP. After becoming enamored with Bitcoin, the three developers resolved to develop a blockchain whose primary function would be to record and verify payments. When Chris Larsen became the group's fourth member in 2012, they immediately went ahead and established a business under the name OpenCoin. Ripple is the name of the company that has emerged in recent times. The three of them collaborated on a post that was published on a Bitcoin forum in 2011 and titled "Bitcoin without Mining." The post was published on Bitcoin.org on May 27, 2011. According to the post, mining Bitcoin results in a significant amount of garbage, which was even described as a side consequence of the system. It stated, "It'll be cool to come up with a Bitcoin that doesn't need miners," and it was cool to think about that possibility. The three of them got to work on constructing a ledger that would be free of these problems. They did had a valid point to make, particularly in light of the fact that Bitcoin is still subject to criticism over its influence on the environment. They chose the name Ripple to convey the idea that its ledger will be spread in a certain manner. Also, possibly to cause 'ripples' in the realm of cryptocurrency. To get things rolling, they distributed a total of 80 billion ripples, also known as XRP, to privately held businesses that were in the race to be formally established. Ripple made its debut on the market with this transaction. It was unique in that its objective was not to entirely upend the pre-existing financial institutions but rather to improve the efficiency with which such systems function. There is a widespread consensus that existing structures and practices must make room for novel concepts and approaches. This viewpoint is reiterated on the organization's official website, xrpl.org, in a passage that reads as follows: "history's most transformative innovations have always relied on the great ideas that came before them—not disrupting them." These financial organizations are able to bridge two different currencies in a matter of seconds by using XRP. Users on either side of the bridge are able to instantly transfer or receive payments in the currency of their respective countries. Anyone who has been through the arduous process of exchanging a foreign fiat currency to their local one, or who has paid significant transaction fees while doing so, will be able to gauge the benefits of what Ripple makes available. Multiply that by the number of transactions of this kind that companies seeking a worldwide reach or banks processing such trades are required to handle. It has a substantial bearing on the outcome. Additionally, it offers a solution to a problem that exists in the real-world finance industry. The XRP Ledger is applicable to a wide variety of business sectors, including, but not limited to, the gaming industry, application development, the music industry, and infrastructure.

Businesses now have the ability to construct a new financial system with the help of BitGo, one that allows them to integrate cryptocurrencies like XRP into their existing infrastructure. In his testimonial for Ripple, the Co-Founder and CEO of a firm named Nium, Prajit Nanu, writes that "Through Nium's use of Ripple in the Philippines and Mexico corridors, we have been able to eliminate pre-funding requirements and offer faster remittances at a lower cost." Ripple's website. According to a further assessment written by Arthit Sriumporn, Senior Vice President of Commercial Banking at Siam Commercial Bank, "Our customers can send money to family and friends overseas in real-time from their phones." Because we are a part of RippleNet, we have been able to completely improve the experience of our customers, grow our business, and ensure that SCB will continue to thrive in the future. A sizable number of companies are currently utilizing the platform in some capacity. It could be due to Ripple's innovative approach to combining the conservative world of banking with the progressive one of cryptocurrency. Ripple is a pioneer in this area. If cryptocurrencies can assist companies, governments, and banks become better and achieve a higher level of customer happiness with decreased costs, then perhaps the adoption and integration of cryptocurrencies would be embraced rather than being repeatedly prohibited by one economy after another time and time again. A step like this would assist in accelerating the world's movement toward all of the potential advances that are already taking place as a result of the many applications of blockchain technology. Additionally, it might bring about a level of stability to the volatile cryptocurrency market, which experiences daily swings in value.

The scalability of XRP is yet another noteworthy aspect of this cryptocurrency. Visa processes approximately 1700 transactions every second on average. The world of blockchain technology is currently engaged in a competition to at least equal such a high speed. Regardless of the revolutionary potential of blockchains, their widespread adoption and expansion in the real world will be hampered if they are cumbersome and time-consuming to operate. Scalability has emerged as a problem just as corporations are beginning to make cautious but steady progress toward acceptance. To get a better picture of how long it takes to complete a transaction using cryptocurrencies versus Visa, let's compare the two. According to the calculations of industry experts, the maximum number of transactions that Bitcoin can process in one second is 4.6. Its processing time is generally agreed to fall somewhere in the range of 3-6 seconds. Ethereum is capable of doing 15. Moreover, XRP outpaces them both with a staggering 1,500 transactions per minute. Simply put, when compared to the top two cryptocurrencies of the present day, it is orders of magnitude faster and more efficient. It's not quite 1700, but it's getting there. That's the goal for Visa. This is regarded as yet another issue that XRP addresses, both for us in the here and now and for blockchains in the foreseeable future.

Let's have a look at some further applications for XRP. Users are able to accept and spend bitcoins from and to any location in the world with the assistance of programs such as BitPay. When it comes to the gaming industry, the use of a program known as FORTE enables game developers to include cryptocurrency and blockchain technology into the codes of the games that they are making. This may make it possible for developers to receive funds directly through their gaming platforms more quickly. For companies, making use of a wide variety of tools like these allows them to reach out to many parts of the economy we have today on a worldwide scale. Ripple makes it easy for individuals to trade currencies with one another and with businesses located in any area of the world. This is in addition to the fact that XRP, along with other cryptocurrencies, can be traded at any moment on the exchange.

The supply of XRP is limited, and all of the tokens that have been created have already been spent. There can never be more than 100 billion XRP available on the market because there are now only that many. At this moment, one XRP is equivalent to 0.92 USD in terms of value. XRP is the third cryptocurrency on the top ten list, after Bitcoin and Ethereum, with a market cap of a remarkable 92 billion dollars. This places XRP in third place. across two million transactions with a total nominal value of seven billion dollars have been executed by Ripple across the RippleNet network. Almost one fifth of all transactions that take place over RippleNet today are conducted through ODL, which utilizes XRP to function as a bridge between two different fiat currencies. Today, ODL went live in four different corridors. Bitso, a Mexican exchange, recently made the announcement that it is processing roughly 10% of remittance payments using ODL, which amounts to $35 billion yearly flows from the United States to Mexico.

The Psychological Pitfalls Of Trading Based Solely On The Direction Of The Market

When traders' emotions are not under control, one of the most significant issues that is related with market mood is the fact that it typically results in greater losses. When traders get thrilled over a major price increase, they frequently are unable to manage their emotions, which results in them making some significant errors along the way. This will lead to another difficulty that many traders experience when trading, which is trading that is too aggressive.

You've probably run into something similar if you've ever watched a trader engage in aggressive trading without first selecting whether to sell or purchase (buy low and sell high), because that trader is likely engaging in a situation similar to this one. When traders make decisions based on their feelings rather than facts, it can put them on a slippery slope that leads to bad decisions and financial losses. It is not easy to keep your emotions in check, but this is something you will need to do at all times if you want to be successful in trading.

When there is an indicator of a market rally, such as a quick jump in the price of an asset, you can expect to see trades that result in a loss occurring. It is very beneficial for market sentiment to push prices upward; however, it is not beneficial if this causes you to lose control of your emotions and trade rashly as a result. Traders will be able to assess how trades are likely to work out before making any decisions based on them when they are able to remove their emotions from the equation and instead focus on the fundamentals that underlie the market.

When this occurs, traders have the opportunity to make the most profitable transactions possible out of any emotions that may be exhibited by the market. However, this is true for any kind of skill, and learning how to handle losing trades is a crucial element of trading. Most traders do not want to lose money due of their own mistakes, but this is true for any kind of skill. It's easy to be swept up in market mood, especially if it makes you feel better about trading rather than predicting the future based on what you've observed in the past. This is especially true if the market sentiment makes you feel better about trading.

The Dangers Inherent in Making Trading Decisions Based on Market Sentiment Only

Trading based on your appraisal of market sentiment is one of the reasons it is not suggested as a strategy since it will come with several complications, which is one of the reasons why it is not advised. The primary difficulty with this is that it is often quite subjective and it is not always straightforward to determine if you are performing each step correctly. I'll break down how traders might approach this in a way that will assist clarify the drawbacks involved with adopting this trading method, so keep reading to find out what the potential problems are while utilizing this strategy.

When trading based on market sentiment, one of the most significant errors you can make is to concentrate all of your attention on price action alone, without balancing out your appraisal of fundamentals as well. This is one of the largest blunders you can do. Because of the impossibility of accurately predicting how future price movements will play out, this tactic, while effective in certain circumstances, should not be considered a foolproof method for making decisions in trading.

This method will frequently result in profitable trades for you, but those trades will not be able to continue indefinitely. In these conditions, it will be challenging to determine precisely what is driving the market and for how much longer it will continue in that capacity. You are not required to keep track of the fundamentals and the figures associated with them. The timing of the dissemination of these fundaments, also known as financial reports, is of utmost significance; therefore, you should pay close attention to it. This is due to the fact that the publication of significant numbers, such as the non-farm payrolls, can have a significant impact on the currency exchange markets, causing an upward trend to quickly reverse and become a downward trend.